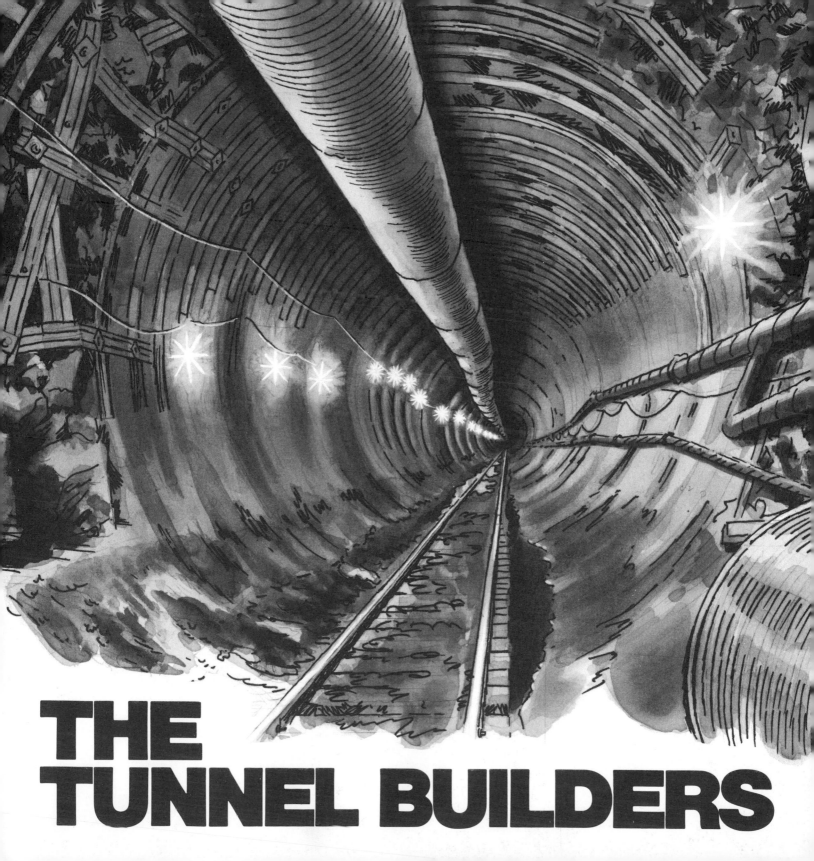

THE TUNNEL BUILDERS

BY
JAMES E. KELLY
AND
WILLIAM R. PARK

DRAWINGS BY
HERBERT E. LAKE

▲ ADDISON-WESLEY

THE TUNNEL

for Jeanne

BUILDERS

Addisonian Press Titles
by James E. Kelly and William R. Park
THE AIRPORT BUILDERS
THE ROADBUILDERS
THE TUNNEL BUILDERS

An Addisonian Press Book

Addison-Wesley Publishing Company, Inc.
Reading, Massachusetts 01867
Printed in the United States of America
First Printing

WZ/WZ   3/76   03721

Library of Congress Cataloging in Publication Data

Kelly, James E
   The tunnel builders.

   SUMMARY: Explains the many techniques used at various
stages of building tunnels under streets and rivers or
through mountains.
   "An Addisonian Press book."
   1. Tunnels—Juvenile literature. 2. Tunneling—
Juvenile literature. [1. Tunnels. 2. Tunneling]
I. Park, William R., joint author. II. Lake,
Herbert E., illus. III. Title.
TA807.K44   624'.19   74-5076
ISBN 0-201-03721-1

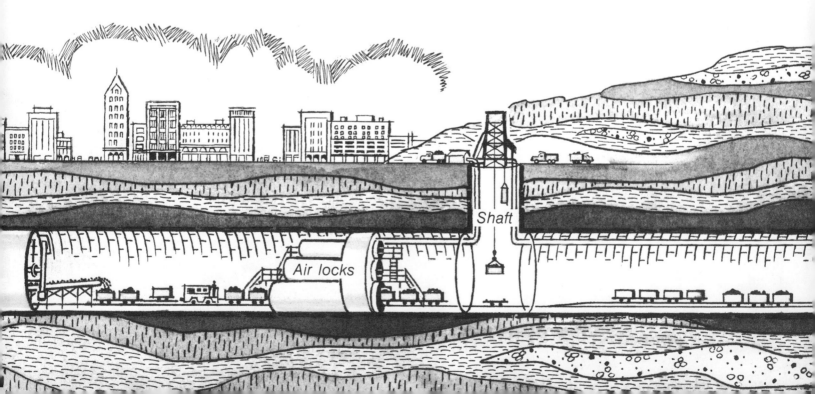

TUNNELS

Some tunnels go through mountains. Some tunnels go through buildings. Some go under streets. Tunnels even go under rivers!

What goes through a tunnel? People, trains, cars and trucks. There are other things, too. Why, even water goes through some tunnels.

And all of these things move more quickly to where they are going because of tunnels.

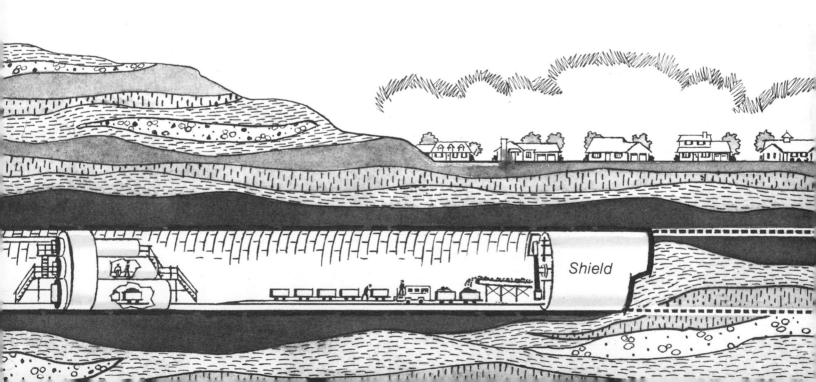

Shield

PLANNING A TUNNEL

The men who plan a tunnel are called *engineers.* The engineers do a lot of work on the tunnel before they start to build it. They learn all about the ground that the tunnel will go through. They are helped by *geologists.* Geologists are people who study soil and rocks that make up the ground.

Special drills are used to drive holes deep in the ground. Dirt and rocks are brought up from the holes. The engineers and geologists study the dirt and rocks. Then the tunnel builders can decide how to dig the tunnel.

Samples of earth and rock are carefully examined.

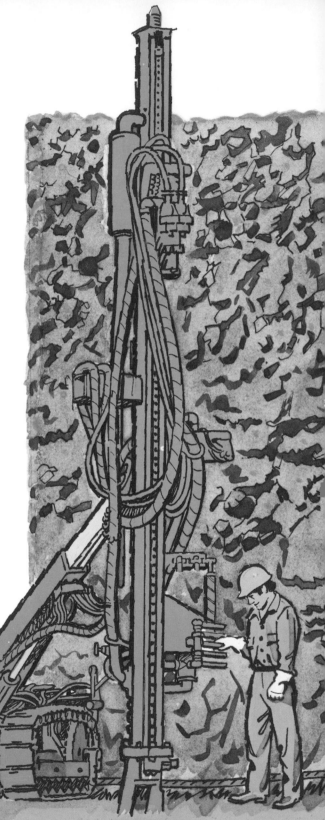

Special drills bring earth and rock samples to the surface.

KINDS OF TUNNELS

Tunnels are built in different shapes. Many times tunnels are round. They are called *circular tunnels.* Circular tunnels are built for going through soft ground or under a river or lake.

Some tunnels are round at the top but square at the bottom. These are called *vertical sidewall tunnels.* The flat floor in these tunnels is used for roads.

Sometimes tunnels are shaped like a horseshoe. *Horseshoe tunnels* are built when the ground is soft but a flat floor is needed.

Another kind of tunnel is the *basket-handle tunnel.* It is a wide tunnel. It is built when two or more roads are needed.

Circular

Vertical sidewall

Circular

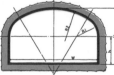
Basket-Handle

Horse shoe

Basket-Handle

THE PARTS OF A TUNNEL

Tunnel builders have names for the different parts of a tunnel.

The top of a tunnel is called the *crown*, or *roof*. Tunnel builders never call it the ceiling!

The floor is called the *invert* by tunnel builders.

The sides of a tunnel are called *sidewalls*.

The *face* is the end of the tunnel where the digging is being done. It is also called the *working face*.

The tunnel entrances are called the *mouths*, or *portals*.

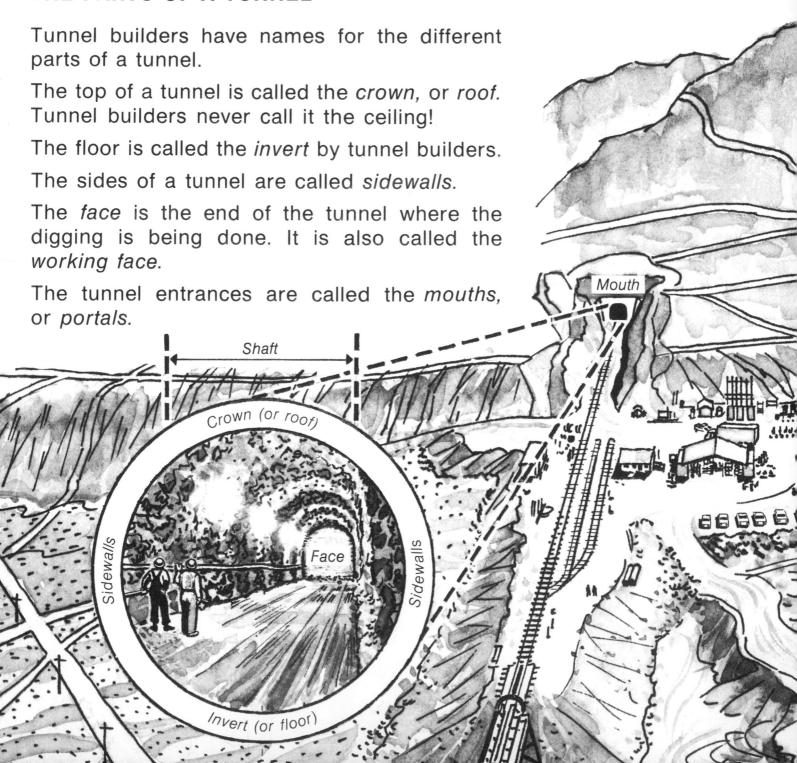

STARTING A TUNNEL

The building equipment is hauled in and out through the open end of the tunnel. Some tunnels are deep underground. Then, men and equipment enter the tunnel through a shaft. The shaft is a hole made straight down from the top of the ground to the tunnel. The tunnel builders sometimes dig the shaft near the middle of the tunnel. Then they can dig the tunnel both ways from there. Now two crews of tunnel builders can work at the same time.

Sometimes, when going through a mountain, a tunnel is started at each end. The two tunnels will meet in the middle of the mountain.

SINKING THE SHAFT

The shaft can be made in several ways. A *clamshell-crane* is used for shafts that are not too deep. It looks like a big machine playing with a Yo-Yo.

The clamshell bucket has huge steel jaws. The jaws pick up dirt from the bottom of the shaft. Then the clamshell-crane lifts the dirt to the surface. There the steel jaws open to drop the dirt into a *dump truck*.

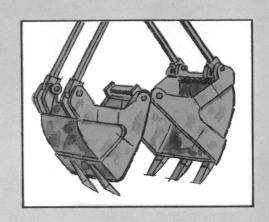

DEEP SHAFTS

Deep shafts are dug a different way. A big steel frame is first built over the top of the shaft.

Dirt and rock are loaded into big steel buckets at the bottom of the shaft. When the buckets are full they are pulled up the shaft by wire ropes. Then the buckets are emptied into a *chute* on the side of the frame.

Dump trucks then drive under the chute. There they are loaded with the dirt and rock to be hauled away.

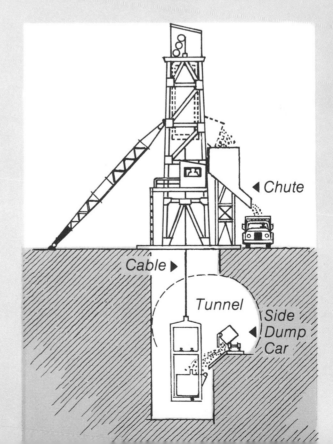

TUNNELING THROUGH ROCK

Sometimes tunnels must go through solid rock. The most common way of building a tunnel through rock is called *blasting and mucking.*

Muck is the broken rock and dirt that must be hauled away as the tunnel is being built. *Mucking* means to clear away all the muck.

Holes are drilled into the rock face. Then the holes are filled with explosives and the rock is blasted. After the smoke has cleared, the muck is removed.

Holes are drilled in the rock face and filled with explosives.

Steel drill bits are used to make the holes.

Conveyor belt moves muck out of tunnel.

Rail mounted drill jumbo

THE DRILL JUMBO

This is how the men begin to tunnel through rock. A big platform on wheels is moved up to the rock face. It is called a *jumbo*. A jumbo may have two or three platforms mounted one above the other. It has many *drills* fastened onto it. These drills reach out in front of the jumbo like steel arms.

On each drill there are steel *bits* that are banged against the rock. The drills with bits attached look like spears. They sound like machine guns when they make holes in the rock.

Truck mounted drill jumbo

Truck mounted rock drills

DRILLING THE ROCK

The holes cannot be drilled just anywhere on the rock face. The holes are carefully drilled in the right places. The way that the holes are spaced on the rock face is called a *drill pattern.*

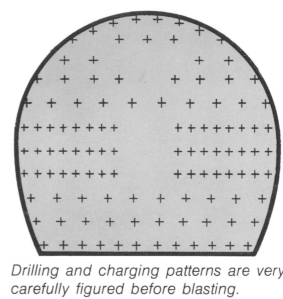

Drilling and charging patterns are very carefully figured before blasting.

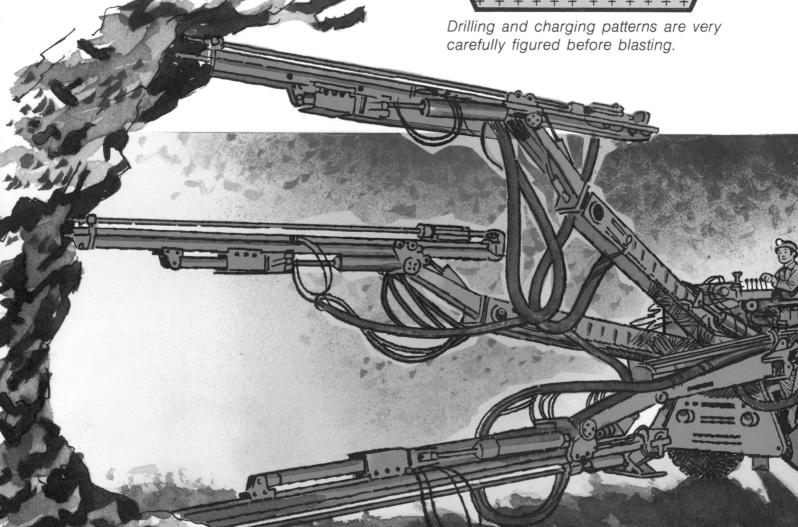

BLASTING THE ROCK

Dynamite is pushed deep into the holes with long wooden poles. When everything is ready, the workmen move away from the rock face.

After everyone is a safe distance away, one of the workmen flips a switch. And the dynamite explodes!

SMOKE TIME

The men do not return to the rock face right after the blast. They must wait until the heat, smoke, and gases from the explosion are gone.

Fresh air is forced through a pipe into the tunnel by big *air pumps.* The heat, smoke, and gases go out of the tunnel through another pipe.

The time that the men wait until it is safe to go back to work is called the *smoke time.*

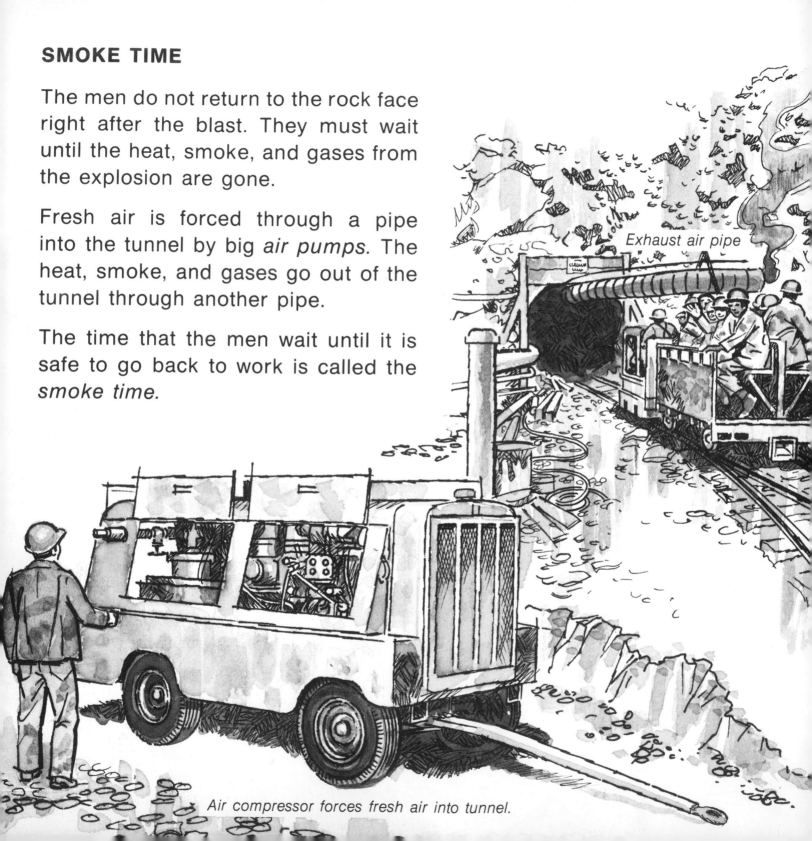

Exhaust air pipe

Air compressor forces fresh air into tunnel.

MUCKING

Now the workmen return to the tunnel. First they will *scale the roof*. This means that they will knock down any loose rock from the roof that might fall on them.

They will also stretch a wire net across the roof. The net will catch any rocks that might fall down later.

After the tunnel is safe, the tunnel builders will move in a *mucking machine*. The mucking machine looks like a small tractor with a big bucket in the front. It scoops up the broken rock and loads it into a *muck train*.

THE MUCK TRAIN

A powerful little engine pulls the muck train to the mouth of the tunnel. When the cars are outside, a special machine turns them upside down to unload the muck.

CONVEYORS

Sometimes the mucking machine loads the muck onto a *conveyor belt.* The muck is first dumped into a metal box called a *hopper.* Doors in the bottom of the hopper drop the muck onto the moving conveyor belt.

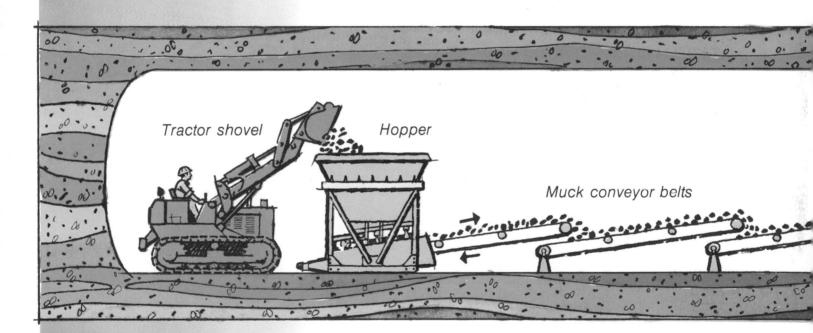

Tractor shovel

Hopper

Muck conveyor belts

A conveyor belt looks like a large, wide rubber band. It slides along over rollers. Several conveyors are put together in a row. This is done when the muck needs to be moved a long way.

TUNNELING MACHINES

Sometimes tunnel builders can dig the tunnel without blasting.

A machine, called a *mole,* may be used. This machine is named after a small animal called the mole. Moles live underground in tunnels that they dig.

A mole machine can dig a tunnel as long as a football field in about two days!

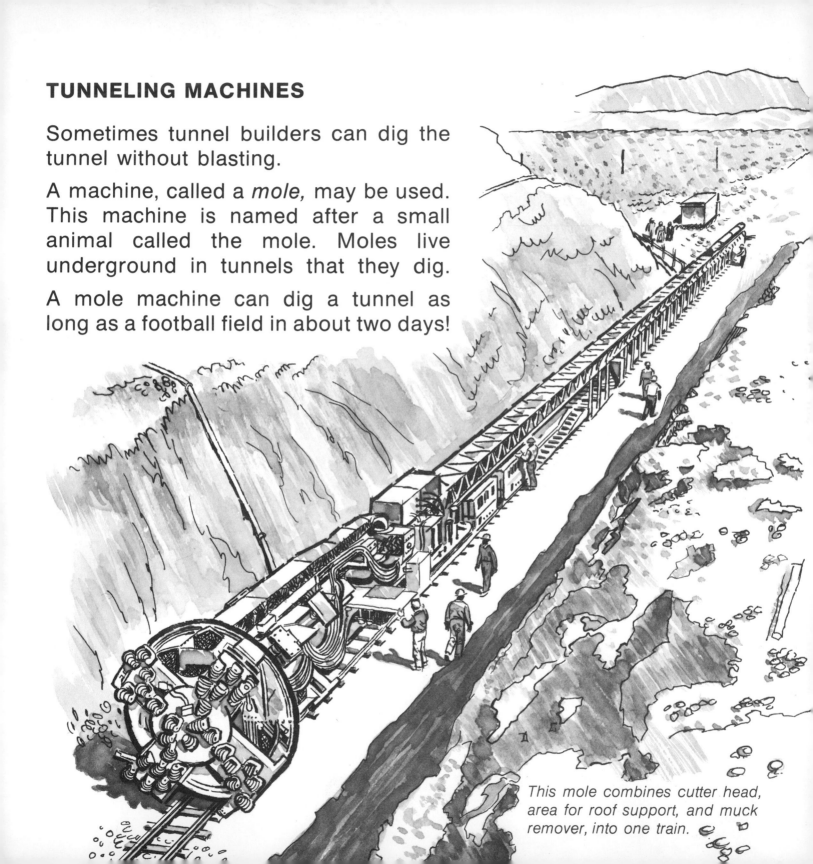

This mole combines cutter head, area for roof support, and muck remover, into one train.

Mole boring machine assembly at job site.

The mole is a big, big machine. At the front is a giant wheel called the *cutter head.* The tunnel will be as big around as the cutter head.

On the front of the cutter head are *teeth.* The teeth are pieces of steel that will rub against the rock.

These teeth cut into the rock. Then the cutter head presses hard against the rock and turns. This makes the rock break into pieces.

TUNNELING MACHINES

Behind the cutter head is a metal tube that has legs reaching down to the floor of the tunnel. These legs can be moved up and down. They point the mole in the right direction.

There are also *side-jacks*. They are stiff steel arms that push out against the sides of the tunnel. The side-jacks

Modern conventional tunnel boring machines work like this. ▼

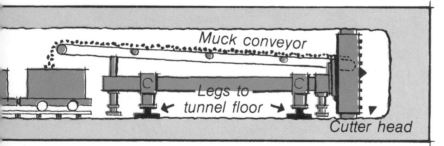

Muck conveyor

Legs to
tunnel floor

Cutter head

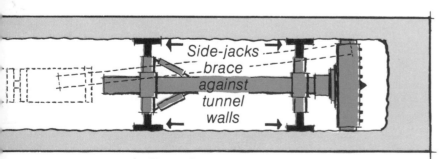

Side-jacks
brace
against
tunnel
walls

▲ *Top view tunnel borer.*

keep the mole from turning as the cutter head turns.

The ground-up rock drops from the cutter head onto a conveyor. It is then dumped into a muck train or onto another conveyor to be hauled out of the tunnel.

New minimole spinning head tunneler for small tunnels goes through hard rock like this. ▼

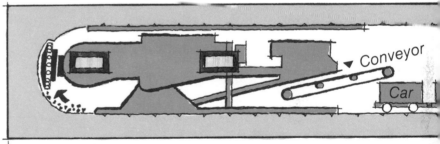

▲ *On the way up cutter head breaks out rock.*

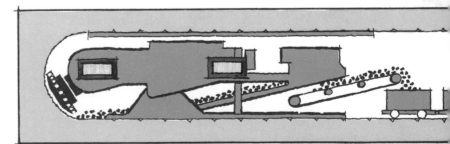

▲ *On the way down cutter head sweeps muck onto conveyor.*

SUPPORTING THE TUNNEL

Digging the hole is just part of building a tunnel. If you tried to dig a hole into a hill of dirt it would be dangerous. Why? The sides and top might cave in.

Tunnel builders build a *support* for their tunnel as they go along.

The support holds the sides and top in place.

Tunnels through dirt need more support than tunnels through rock. But even rock tunnels have to be supported to make them safe.

SUPPORTING TUNNELS WITH STEEL RIBS

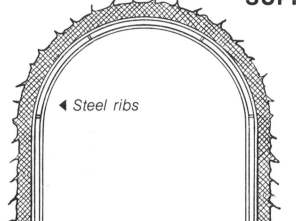

◀ *Steel ribs*

Often tunnel builders put up steel braces, called *ribs.* These support the tunnel. They are placed several feet apart all along the tunnel.

The ribs are held in place by steel rods and wooden blocks. The rods and blocks connect the ribs to each other.

Tunnel face

Blocks ▼

Rods ▼

Blocks ▼

Rods ▲

◀ Ribs ▶

◀ Ribs ▶

SUPPORTING TUNNELS WITH ROOF BOLTS

Sometimes *roof bolts* are used to hold up the roof of tunnels built through rock. The roof bolt is a long steel rod.

A hole is first drilled into the rock above the tunnel. Next the roof bolt is pushed up into the hole.

The end that is pushed into the rock gets bigger when the bolt is twisted. This holds it tight inside the hole.

Then a piece of steel with a hole in it is placed on the outside end of the bolt. This flat piece is held firmly against the tunnel roof by twisting a nut on the outside end of the roof bolt.

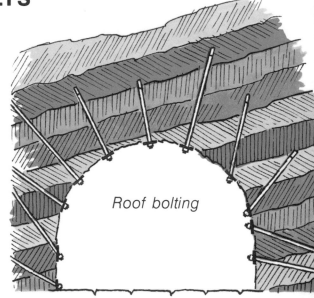

Roof bolting

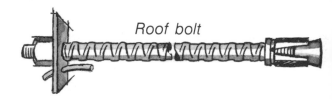

Roof bolt

Installing rock bolts using jumbo.

Tensiling the bolt.

CONCRETE SUPPORTS

There is another way that tunnel builders support a tunnel through rock. They spray the inside of the tunnel with concrete.

A pump forces the concrete through a big hose. Two men stand on a jumbo and spray the walls and roof. When they are finished, the concrete is about four inches thick.

TUNNELING THROUGH SOFT GROUND

Often a tunnel goes through soft ground. Special care is taken to keep the ground from caving in. There are many ways to do this.

Sometimes pointed boards are driven around the roof and sidewalls of the tunnel. Then the dirt is dug away.

Another way to dig through soft ground is to drive steel plates ahead of the tunnel. These plates will hold up the roof while the men dig away the dirt. If the dirt is *very* soft, it is held back by *breast boards*. These boards are braced against the working face.

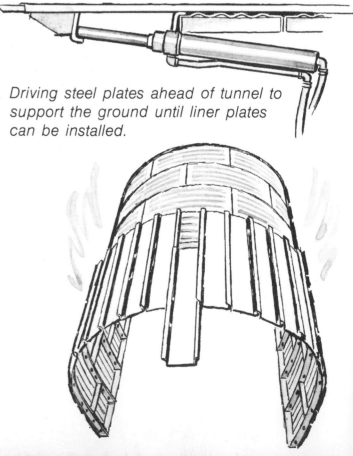

Driving steel plates ahead of tunnel to support the ground until liner plates can be installed.

DIGGING THE DIRT

Sometimes men dig the dirt away from the working face with shovels. If the dirt is very hard to dig, then *air spades* will be used instead.

These air spades work and sound like rock drills on a jumbo. But they do not have a long steel bit on the end. Air spades have a small flat shovel.

As the dirt is dug away, the tunnel must be supported to keep it from caving in.

Digging with air spade.

Heading and upper breast boards hold loose dirt back.

SUPPORTING THE SOFT GROUND

Soft ground can be supported with steel *liner plates* or with *steel ribs*.

Liner plates are sheets of steel that are curved. When they are bolted together they form a steel tube the same size as the inside of the tunnel. An *erector arm* is sometimes used to hold the plates in place until they are bolted together.

Steel ribs are sometimes used. They are like the ones used to support rock tunnels. After the ribs have been put in place, big wooden boards are wedged in between the ribs and the top of the tunnel.

Installing liner plates.

Erector arm holds liner plates in position until men bolt them in.

Boards wedged on rib tops.

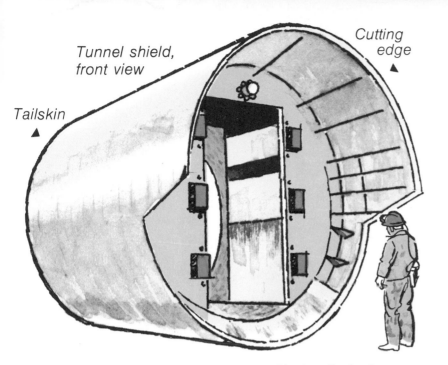

Tunnel shield, front view

Tailskin

Cutting edge

TUNNELING WITH SHIELDS

Digging at tunnel face under protection of shield.

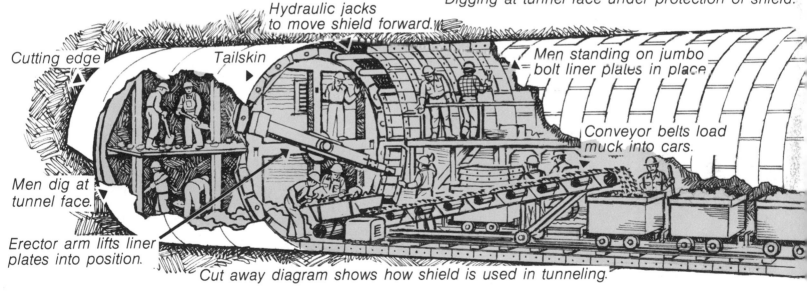

Cutting edge

Tailskin

Hydraulic jacks to move shield forward.

Men standing on jumbo bolt liner plates in place.

Conveyor belts load muck into cars.

Men dig at tunnel face.

Erector arm lifts liner plates into position.

Cut away diagram shows how shield is used in tunneling.

Some tunnels are *shield driven.* The shield is like a very large tin can with both ends open. The shield is pushed through soft ground by *thrust jacks.*

The front edge of the shield is called the *cutting edge.* The back part is called the *tailskin.*

As the shield moves forward, the tunnel lining is built behind the tailskin. The lining can be steel liner plates or concrete or stone.

TUNNELING WITH SHIELDS

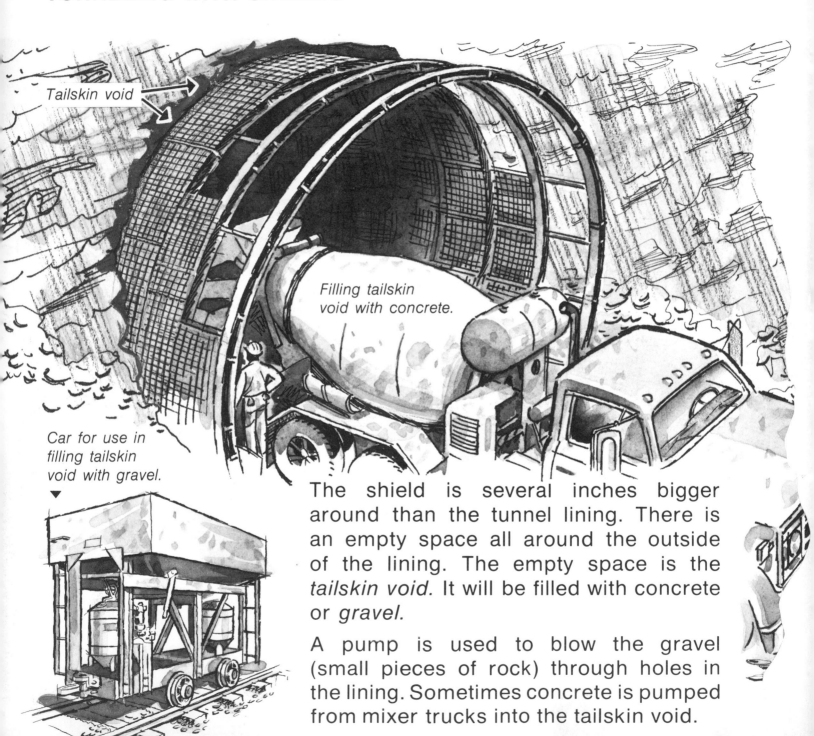

Tailskin void

Filling tailskin void with concrete.

Car for use in filling tailskin void with gravel.

The shield is several inches bigger around than the tunnel lining. There is an empty space all around the outside of the lining. The empty space is the *tailskin void.* It will be filled with concrete or *gravel.*

A pump is used to blow the gravel (small pieces of rock) through holes in the lining. Sometimes concrete is pumped from mixer trucks into the tailskin void.

Sometimes there is water in the ground that the tunnel passes through. The water must be kept out of the tunnel.

Water-soaked soil can be found almost anywhere. The tunnel builders often run into underground rivers or pockets of dirt filled with water. Of course, water is most often found when tunneling through sandy soil under a river or lake.

The tunnel builders who work in wet and sandy soil are called *sandhogs*.

USING AIR TO KEEP WATER OUT

One of the best ways to keep water out of the tunnel is to pump air into it. This is done with an *air compressor* that blows air into the tunnel.

The air is forced into the tunnel. There is so much air that it is pressing out just as hard as the water is pressing in.

This air pressure will keep the water out and the inside of the tunnel dry.

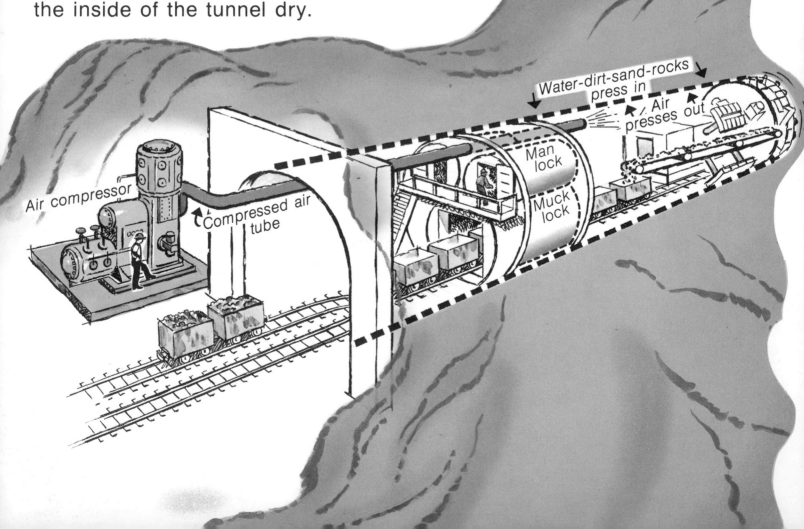

Air compressor

Compressed air tube

Man lock

Muck lock

Water-dirt-sand-rocks press in

Air presses out

AIR LOCKS

The compressed air in the tunnel is called *low air.* It is kept in the tunnel by an *air lock.* An air lock is shaped like a large tin can. It has a door at each end. The doors close so tightly that air cannot go through them. The air lock is big. It fills the tunnel and separates the low air inside the tunnel from the outside air.

If a man wants to enter the tunnel, he enters the air lock and closes the door behind him. The air pressure in the air lock is changed. It is made the same as the air pressure inside the tunnel. Then the man can safely enter the tunnel through the inside door.

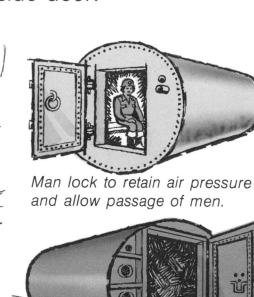

Man lock to retain air pressure and allow passage of men.

Muck lock to pass muck cars.

THE EMERGENCY LOCK

If the tunnel is below a river or lake, there may be a special air lock near the top of the tunnel. It is called an *emergency lock.*

If the air pressure in the tunnel gets too low, water and mud may suddenly pour in. The sandhogs then run to the emergency lock. When everyone is in the lock, the door (called the inside door) is closed and the water and mud shut out. Then the sandhogs escape through the other door (called the outside door).

OTHER WAYS TO KEEP THE WATER OUT

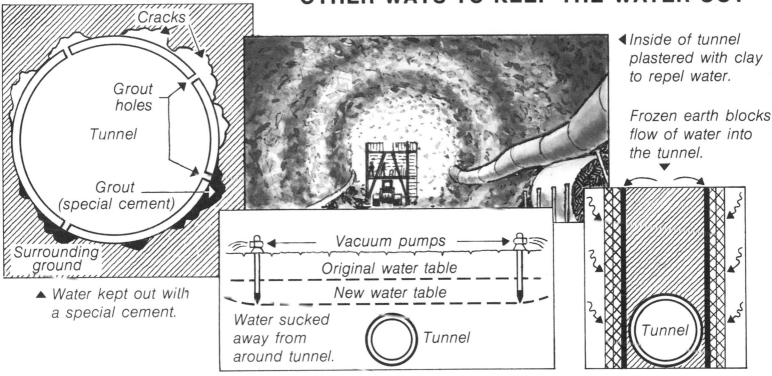

Cracks

Grout holes

Tunnel

Grout (special cement)

Surrounding ground

▲ Water kept out with a special cement.

◄ Inside of tunnel plastered with clay to repel water.

Frozen earth blocks flow of water into the tunnel.
▼

Vacuum pumps

Original water table

New water table

Water sucked away from around tunnel.

Tunnel

Tunnel

There are other ways of keeping water out of a tunnel. Sometimes cracks in the rock and soil can be filled with a special cement. This keeps the water from leaking into the tunnel. Or the inside of the tunnel might be plastered with clay.

If the tunnel is not too deep, water may be pumped away from the ground around the tunnel. Long pipes are driven in the ground. *Pumps* are placed on the top of the pipes. The water is then sucked away from the ground and up through the pipes.

Sometimes the tunnel builders freeze the water and wet dirt around a tunnel! *Refrigeration pipes* are driven deep into the ground around the tunnel. This frozen material can be dug like solid rock.

LINING THE TUNNEL WITH CONCRETE

The men have finished digging the tunnel. But it is not yet ready to be used. Another *lining* must be put on the inside of the tunnel. This lining will keep dirt and rocks from falling into the tunnel. It will keep water out, too.

When the men were digging the tunnel, they put up one lining. This first lining kept the tunnel from caving in. It was called the *primary lining.*

The new lining is called the *secondary lining.* Steel bars are wired together and then covered with concrete to make the secondary lining.

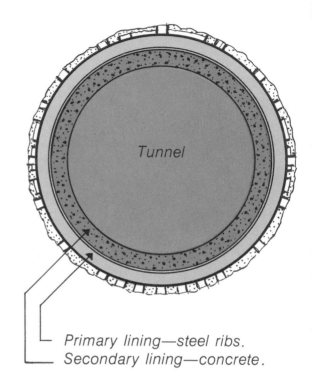

Tunnel

Primary lining—steel ribs.
Secondary lining—concrete.

Tunnel with primary lining in place.
Secondary concrete lining to be installed.

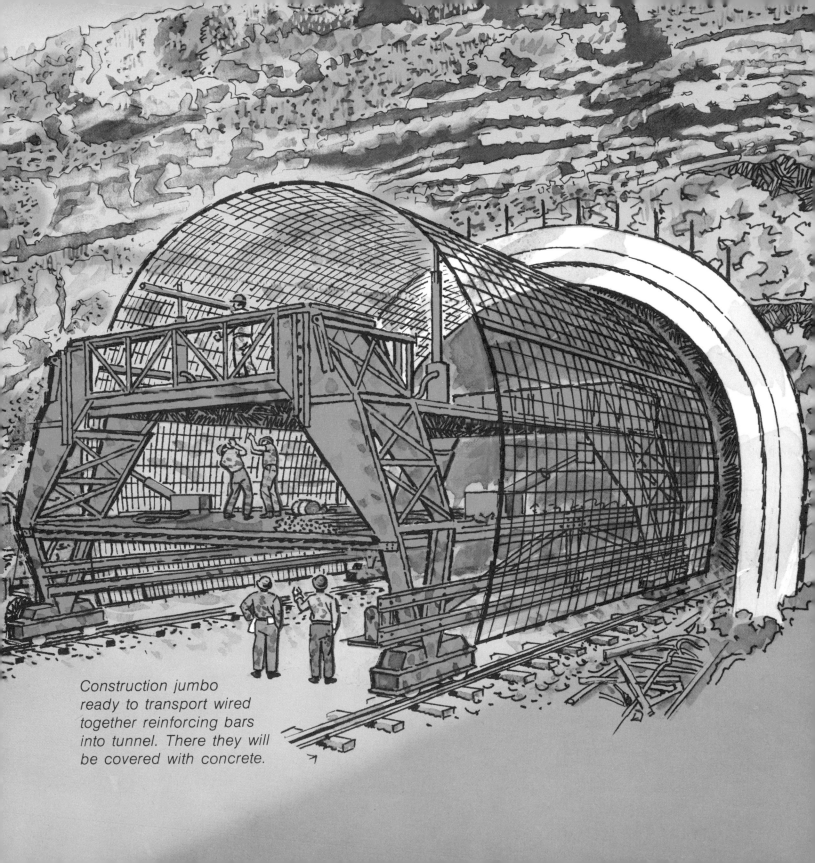

Construction jumbo ready to transport wired together reinforcing bars into tunnel. There they will be covered with concrete.

LINING THE TUNNEL WITH CONCRETE

Concrete mixing plant

The concrete is made by mixing sand and water and cement together in a *mixing plant.* The wet concrete is loaded into trucks going to the tunnel. There, the concrete is dumped onto a conveyor belt or into mine cars.

The concrete is then spread on the tunnel floor or pumped through a pipe and sprayed on the roof and sidewalls.

Workmen smooth out the concrete with *hand trowels.*

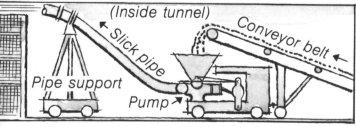

(Inside tunnel)

Slick pipe

Conveyor belt

Pipe support

Pump

Spraying concrete over top and sides of tunnel lining.

Using hand trowel to smooth out wet concrete on tunnel floor.

U. S. 1902421

The wet concrete is held in place by *concrete forms.* After the concrete dries, it is hard and strong. Then the forms can be removed.

Forms are made of steel or wood. They are the same shape as the inside of the tunnel. A jumbo places them inside the tunnel. A small space is left between the forms and the tunnel roof and side-walls. Wet concrete is then pumped into this space.

Steel forms are covered with wood or wire mesh to hold concrete until it sets.

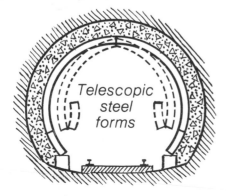

Telescopic steel forms

Wet concrete is held against tunnel walls by steel or wood forms. After concrete has "set" forms are collapsed, moved forward and the operation is repeated.

LINING THE TUNNEL WITH CONCRETE

When the concrete is hard, the forms are moved. Then the jumbo is rolled forward. The forms are used again to put the concrete lining on the next part of the tunnel.

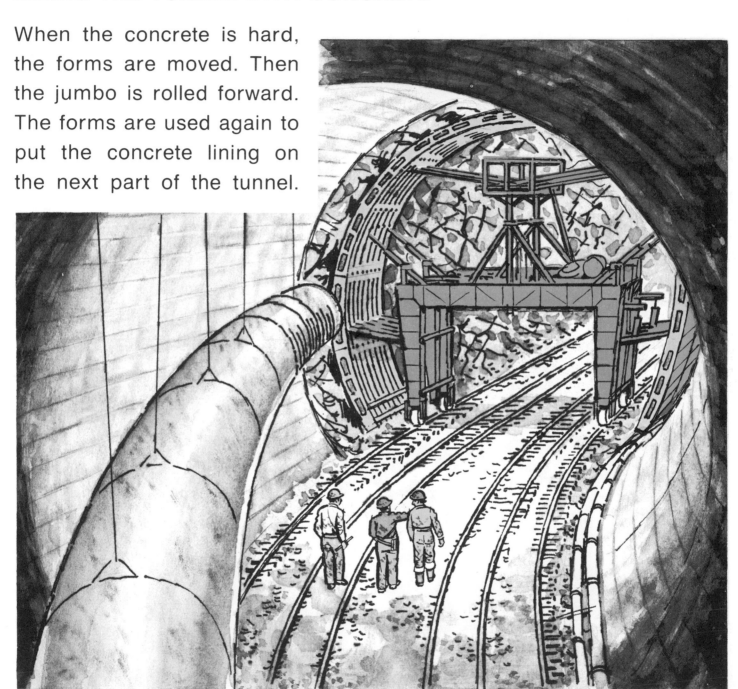

Conventional form carried by jumbo traveler.

VENTILATING THE TUNNEL

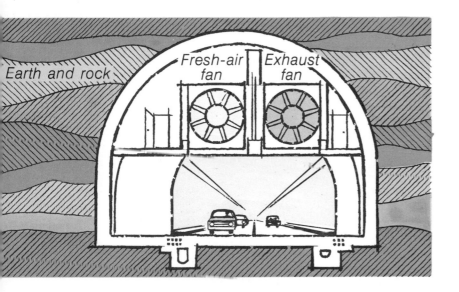

If cars, buses, or trains go through the tunnel, the poisonous fumes from their engines must be removed. Giant fans pull the poisonous fumes out of the tunnel. They are called *exhaust fans.*

Other giant fans push fresh air into the tunnel. They are called *fresh-air fans.*

These two kinds of fans are *ventilating fans.* They are placed in shafts or at the opening of the tunnel.

▲ Giant fans push fresh or exhaust air through pipes and ducts.

▲ Diagram shows direction taken by fresh and exhaust air as forced by fans.

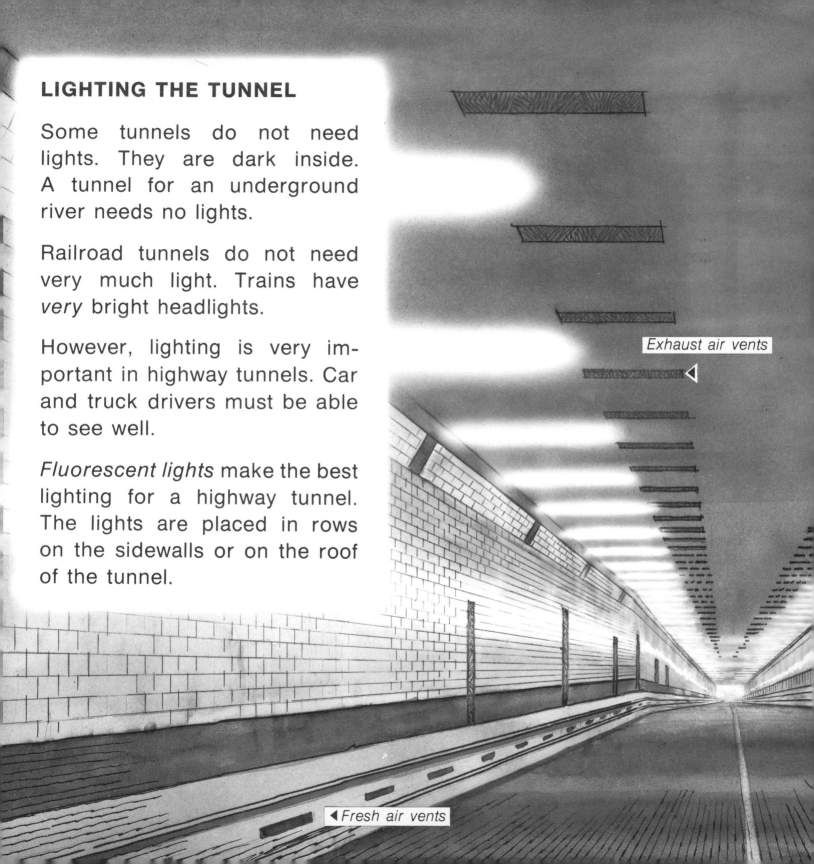

LIGHTING THE TUNNEL

Some tunnels do not need lights. They are dark inside. A tunnel for an underground river needs no lights.

Railroad tunnels do not need very much light. Trains have *very* bright headlights.

However, lighting is very important in highway tunnels. Car and truck drivers must be able to see well.

Fluorescent lights make the best lighting for a highway tunnel. The lights are placed in rows on the sidewalls or on the roof of the tunnel.

Exhaust air vents

◀ Fresh air vents

READY TO SERVE PEOPLE FOR MANY YEARS

It has taken a long time to build a tunnel. Maybe years! A new tunnel will make traveling and moving things easier and quicker.

Tunnels are built to be used for many, many years. No one knows just how long a tunnel will last. Some have lasted for thousands of years.

Tunnels built today should last even longer, because they are built better and stronger.

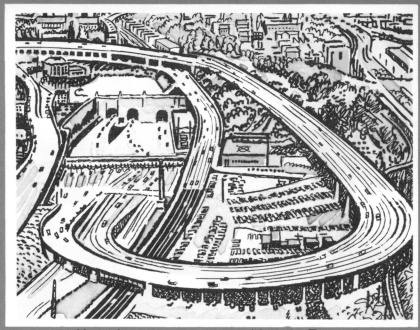

New Jersey entrance to Lincoln Tunnel

Chicago subway system station

San Jacinto Tunnel for Colorado River water

6 mile long Moffat railroad tunnel through the Rocky Mountains

Eisenhower Memorial Tunnel, Colorado

Holland Tunnel under Hudson River, New York

Union Canal Tunnel—oldest tunnel in U.S.

About the Authors

The authors of THE TUNNEL BUILDERS are two men active in the construction industry. With the help of their wives—both experienced teachers—their expertise was directed to young readers.

James E. Kelly is educational director of the Heavy Constructors Association of Greater Kansas City, a chapter of the Associated General Contractors of America. Interested in government, Mr. Kelly is currently serving as president of the Kansas City International Relations Council to study foreign affairs. He and his wife live in Independence, Missouri.

William R. Park is principal construction economist at Midwest Research Institute. He is a licensed professional engineer, active in the American Society of Civil Engineers and other technical and professional organizations. Mr. Park is the author of two technical books and more than a hundred articles for construction journals. He and his two young sons live in Prairie Village, Kansas.

About the Artist

Herbert E. Lake attended the Art Students League in New York City. Later he opened his own studio in Kansas City and has earned an enviable reputation in his chosen field. Mr. Lake lives in Prairie Village, Kansas.